THE LOVE EVERYBODY WANTS

How to Build Your Relationships on God's Love

BIBLE STUDY GUIDE + STREAMING VIDEO
FOUR SESSIONS

Madison Prewett Troutt

The Love Everybody Wants Study Guide

© 2023 by Madison Prewett Troutt

Requests for information should be addressed to:
HarperChristian Resources, 3900 Sparks Dr. SE, Grand Rapids, Michigan 49546

ISBN 978-0-310-16061-8 (softcover)
ISBN 978-0-310-16062-5 (ebook)

Scripture quotations are taken from The Holy Bible, New International Version®, NIV®. Copyright© 1973, 1978, 1984, 2011 by Biblica, Inc.® Used by permission of Zondervan. All rights reserved worldwide. www.Zondervan.com. The "NIV" and "New International Version" are trademarks registered in the United States Patent and Trademark Office by Biblica, Inc.®

Any internet addresses (websites, blogs, etc.) and telephone numbers in this study guide are offered as a resource. They are not intended in any way to be or imply an endorsement by HarperChristian Resources, nor does HarperChristian Resources vouch for the content of these sites and numbers for the life of this study guide.

All rights reserved. No portion of this book may be reproduced, stored in a retrieval system, or transmitted in any form or by any means—electronic, mechanical, photocopy, recording, scanning, or other—except for brief quotations in critical reviews or articles, without the prior written permission of the publisher.

HarperChristian Resources titles may be purchased in bulk for church, business, fundraising, or ministry use. For information, please email ResourceSpecialist@ChurchSource.com.

Author is represented by the literary agency of The FEDD Agency, Inc., Post Office Box 341973, Austin, Texas 78734.

First Printing September 2023 / Printed in the United States of America

23 24 25 26 27 LBC 5 4 3 2 1

Contents

Session One

Who and Why

5

Session Two

Conviction and Confidence

29

Session Three

Patterns, Purpose, and Peace

57

Session Four

Stand Firm and Surrender

85

About the Author

113

SESSION ONE

WHO AND WHY

all together

Welcome to the Session One group section! This section is designed for a group to use together. To get the most out of your discussion time, review the discussion questions in advance and **start with the questions most relevant to your group.** You don't have to push through every single question. There are suggested time limits for each activity—use a timer if you need one! Have your Bibles out and ready to reference.

THE LOVE EVERYBODY WANTS

hey again! (5 minutes)

Before you begin your study, read this note from Madi quietly to yourselves.

It's so good to see you here. It's a gift to be able to meet you in this content and talk about a topic that is important to both of us: love.

When I was thinking about this topic, I wanted to include "everybody" in the title because it's not an exaggeration. Everybody wants to be loved—everybody. And we look for love everywhere: from families to significant others, to friendships, to off-and-on-again relationships, to followers. But love—real love—can't be found in any of those places if you look there first. Maybe you have realized this already from experience. But the truth is there is a love that satisfies our desires. There is a love that we should be after. A love that lasts. A love that changes everything. The love everybody wants. The love you were made for.

So, let's get started.

Madi

SESSION ONE • WHO AND WHY

let's pray

Group leader, read the following prayer over your group.

God, You are love, and You created us in love and for love.
We ask, Lord, that You enlighten the eyes of our hearts
that we might see You and understand Your Word
and seek You above all else. Give us wisdom from
Your truths, fill us with a desire to faithfully follow after You.
Soften our hearts, God. Forgive us for chasing after the wrong
loves and choosing other things and people over You.
You are far greater than anything else this world can offer us.

Help us. We need You, God.

press play

Session One: Who and Why (19 minutes)

As you watch the Session One video, use the space below to write down thoughts, quotes, and questions.

video notes

→ The greatest commandment

→ Complete in Christ, confident in ourselves, connected to a community

→ On a scale of one to ten, one being terrible and ten being the absolute best, how would you rate your relationship with God?

1   10

→ How would you rate your relationship with yourself?

1   10

SESSION ONE • WHO AND WHY

→ What about your relationship with others, including the opposite sex?

→ The creation story is a love story.

→ Sin was strong, but His love was stronger.

→ Times I feel affirmed and loved

THE LOVE EVERYBODY WANTS

talk it out (20 minutes)

Group leader, ask the group these questions and work through them together.

1. Before we can begin growing in our relationship with God, we must be aware of where we are starting. Circle a few words from the list below that best describe how you feel when you think about God.

ashamed	distant	lukewarm	full of life	loved
ungrateful	angry	hesitant	purposeful	accepted
absent	overwhelmed	confused	peaceful	free
silent	tense	constrained	fathered	known
judged	disappointed	difficult	constant	empowered

Have each person in the group share one word they circled and, if they want to, give a brief explanation of why they chose that word.

SESSION ONE • WHO AND WHY

2. Choose a volunteer to read **Genesis 1:27-28**. Notice the verbs in the verses. What did God do that expressed love for His creation? How did the very first humans experience and express love—to God and to each other?

3. In **Genesis 3:1-5**, the Enemy tempts Eve to eat the one fruit in the garden that God said she couldn't eat. The Enemy deceives Eve, saying, "For God knows that when you eat from it your eyes will be opened, and you will be like God, knowing good and evil." What was the lie about God that the Enemy led Eve to believe? How does knowing God's character give us encouragement and strength against the Enemy's lies? Discuss ways you can know God's character more deeply.

picture this
Don't Miss This Chance! (15 minutes)

Group leader, read this note from Madi to everyone.

I am a visual learner. When I read the Bible, I like to picture myself in the scene—sometimes I'm someone in the crowd or someone Jesus is responding to or healing. It helps me apply Scripture to my own life. Although times might look different now than it did thousands of years ago, nothing has changed when it comes to us all needing Jesus.

The Gospels—the books of Matthew, Mark, Luke, and John—record what Jesus said and did while He was on earth. Passages from the Gospels reveal Jesus, and, in a way, give us an opportunity to *see* Him.

This week, you're going to read the passage about the greatest commandment together. This story is the heartbeat of this study. Everything we'll be talking about from here on out can be traced back to these verses. Take this opportunity to let Jesus' words change you—do you want to live your life in line with His priorities? In these few words, Jesus tells you how to start living out the life He wants for you—a life rooted in His eternal, unchanging love.

Jesus gave an incredible response to those testing Him and judging Him, when they asked Him: "What is the greatest commandment?"

Imagine what you would be hearing and seeing if you were right there in the story. What does Jesus look like? How does He respond to those who misunderstand Him? What does the tone of His voice sound like? Does He use His hands when He talks? If you were there, what would you see?

SESSION ONE • WHO AND WHY

Group leader, read this week's gospel passage aloud.

> Hearing that Jesus had silenced the Sadducees, the Pharisees got together. One of them, an expert in the law, tested him with this question: "Teacher, which is the greatest commandment in the Law?"
>
> Jesus replied: "'Love the Lord your God with all your heart and with all your soul and with all your mind.' This is the first and greatest commandment. And the second is like it: 'Love your neighbor as yourself.' All the Law and the Prophets hang on these two commandments."
>
> **Matthew 22:34-40**

Reflect on this gospel passage using the following prompts. If you have time, discuss these questions out loud. You could break into groups and share, or just write them down individually.

→ What did you see? Check any that apply.

- ☐ Jesus
- ☐ a disagreement
- ☐ a call to purpose
- ☐ a crowd

What else? Write it down.

→ How does this story challenge you?

→ Why do you think "love" is God's greatest command? And why do we often turn to other loves before we turn to His love?

SESSION ONE • WHO AND WHY

until next time (5 minutes)

Use this space to write down all the names of the people in your group. Refer back to this section to pray for everyone by name throughout the week.

_____
_____
_____
_____

When's the next meeting?

_____

Group leader, close your time with the following prayer.

God, You made each of us uniquely and intentionally and You love us deeply. We are longing for love, and we've run after it in so many different directions. Your love is the love that we want. Your love is the only love that satisfies. I pray that our greatest priority would be to love You with all of our heart, soul, and strength. This week, speak to us, reveal Yourself to us, and show us more of who You are as we seek You with all our heart.

In Jesus' name,

15

ON YOUR OWN

Part 1

checking in

Hey—it's Madi. Thanks for showing up for the personal study. No matter where you are in your faith journey, I am so glad you are here. There are no wrong answers. There is no shame in being where you are—God meets you right where you are, but He loves you too much to leave you there. He wants you to grow in relationship with Him! Even though I've been on this journey for a long time, I am far from perfect and daily seek to know God more, so I make it a priority to follow the same disciplines I'm going to talk about. By His grace, I want to keep growing in my faith.

Throughout this personal study section, you'll have opportunities to study Scripture, challenge yourself, pray Scripture, and reflect on what you've learned. I've found these practices transformative in my own journey, and I hope they help you, too. Are you already spending time with God daily?

No matter what your answer is to that question, I want you to spend five extra minutes each day with God throughout this study. The exercises in these pages can guide the added time. I hope that you continue spending time with God daily long after this study is over, but right now, focus on today. **Don't push through every single question just to fill in the blanks.** If one of the activities is meaningful for you, whether it's a longer passage of Scripture, a weekly challenge, or a verse to take to prayer, allow yourself to spend time on it.

Let's do this together!

Invite His Holy Spirit into your personal study with this prayer:

God, please send Your Holy Spirit to guide me during this time of prayer and study. I want to grow in my understanding of Your great love for me—Your love is the love that I want the most.

Let's get a picture of your life right now by revisiting what we talked about during the group time. Where did you place yourself on these scales? Below each scale, write a few words about why you chose that number.

On a scale of one to ten with ten being the absolute best...

How would you rate your relationship with God?

How would you rate your relationship with yourself?

Last, what about your relationships with others?

No matter what rating you gave your relationship with God, there will always be room for improvement. We are always growing! The hope is that through this study those numbers increase, not only going higher, but deeper. In this session, we're going to focus on our relationship with God. Prayer is one of my favorite ways to connect with God. Prayer is time with Him—time spent talking to Him and revealing your heart to Him, time spent listening for His voice and just sitting in silence with Him. Setting aside daily time for prayer helps you comprehend His great love for you.

You already have this love—prayer is a beautiful way to experience it more deeply. Prayer is most impactful when it isn't something we do every once in a while, but when it's a lifestyle and priority. But how do we pray? What do we even say? These are good questions, and I've got a few answers.

FIND A TIME

Don't just say "I'll pray in the morning." Pick a time and faithfully keep it. Jesus got up early in the morning. For me, I always pray in the morning and at night right before bed. Pick a time that works best for your schedule and try to stick to it.

FIND A PLACE

Jesus had a specific place He went to pray. I have realized for me, I am more consistent in my prayer life when I know the time and place. I begin to look forward to it. I have a prayer closet I pray in every morning or if for some reason I am running behind, I will use the time I have in my car while driving to pray. Find a place—removed from distractions—and pray out loud.

FIND A POSTURE

I mean this literally and figuratively. Find a position, whether it be sitting, kneeling, standing, or a combination. But also a heart posture: one of surrender, humility, holiness, and gratitude. I always like to start my prayers by thanking God (Psalm 100).

FIND A PLAN

This sounds more intense than I mean for it to. My prayer life has become personal and powerful because every time I spend time with God, I go in with a plan. I don't just ramble or talk about what I need God to do for me. I pray for those who don't know Jesus and the hurting and suffering. I pray for leaders in position of influence, for my friends, and my family. I spend time worshipping God and listening. I spend time praying Scripture. If praying out loud or for longer than a minute is new for you, I would encourage you to start with the Lord's Prayer (Matthew 6:9–13).

Prayer doesn't have to take you a whole hour, especially as you start your prayer journey. Even if all you have is five minutes for undivided attention and heartfelt prayers to God, that is great! Hopefully as we grow together in our prayer life, we find a way to make more time for what matters to us most, like prayer.

My prayer for you this week is that through time with Him, you experience His love for you with a new depth.

Part 2
in His Word: Study Scripture

Let's read this passage together: **1 John 4:8–12**

You can hear from God every day. Second Timothy 3:16 reminds us that "all scripture is God-breathed." Listening to His words gives us more insight into His incredible love for us. I love this letter that John wrote. John was one of the original twelve disciples. He walked and talked with Jesus, and he would have heard Jesus explain the greatest commandment. Here, John spoke beautifully to other Christians about love. Not surprisingly, it lines up with what Jesus said in Matthew 22:36–40.

This passage is yours to explore. Highlight phrases that make you curious. Underline words that you want to remember throughout the day. Write questions in the margins.

> Whoever does not love does not know God, because God is love. This is how God showed his love among us: He sent his one and only Son into the world that we might live through him. This is love: not that we loved God, but that he loved us and sent his Son as an atoning sacrifice for our sins. Dear friends, since God so loved us, we also ought to love one another. No one has ever seen God; but if we love one another, God lives in us and his love is made complete in us.

→ Where does love come from? Who loves first? How does that perspective line up with or conflict with explanations about love that you've heard before?

→ Which specific phrases in this passage remind you of the greatest commandment **(Matthew 22:36–40)**?

→ God loved first—His love for us isn't based on anything that we have or have not done. How does this truth shape your understanding of His love for you and the kind of love that you can offer to others?

SESSION ONE • WHO AND WHY

Part 3
weekly challenge:
Seek God First

> Very early in the morning, while it was still dark, Jesus got up, left the house and went off to a solitary place, where he prayed.
>
> **Mark 1:35**

Each week, I'm going to offer you a challenge that will help you grow in your relationship with Christ. My challenge to you this week is to write out a plan for some time with Jesus. This isn't another box to check—making time for Him is a response to His love for you. Remember what Jesus said in **Matthew 22:37**: "Love the Lord your God with all your heart and with all your soul and with all your mind."

Having a brief time with Jesus at the beginning of the day is a great way to direct your heart, soul, and mind to Him right away. When you make time for Him in your day, you are following the greatest commandment. Love for yourself and love for others is completely dependent on your love for God. If you're not creating space to experience God's love yourself, you're not going to have anything to offer anyone else. Time with God is the source of love—if you're not taking that chance to get love straight from the Source, you will be running on empty!

I've found that planning this time in the morning, very first thing, is super helpful. Maybe this makes you feel wary—after all, so many of us have tried

23

to put together a Bible-reading and prayer morning routine and found ourselves just hitting snooze. But responding to God's love looks like trying again, even if we've failed before.

Plan out at least one specific time with God this week. You can plan out this time using the chart below, or you can make a similar chart in your own planner or journal.

Example: Madi's Plan Date: (10/25)	My Plan Date: (____ /____)
Time: at 5:30 a.m.	Time: _____
Length: for 10 minutes	Length: _____
Place: in my prayer closet	Place: _____
Posture: on my knees	Posture: _____
Attitude: in gratitude	Attitude: _____
Plan: praying Scripture (Psalm 23)	Plan: _____

No matter what else is going on in your life, come to prayer with gratitude. You have so much to be thankful for that you may not even realize. Even if you are not happy with who you are or where you are right now, you can be grateful for anything God has given you. Salvation? Breath in your lungs? Freedom? A bed? Pray to the One who loves you—the One who wants to hear every single word!

My hope is that this challenge will help you get to know God. His love is the foundation of all other loves.

SESSION ONE • WHO AND WHY

Part 4
to His heart:
Prayer and Worship

When we acknowledge God's love as our foundation, Scripture becomes very personal to us. Through prayer and Scripture, we can understand His love for us more deeply and become more secure in it. Even though they were written long before we were alive, the words of Scripture are for all believers. So, with great confidence, we can bring God's Word into our prayers, repeating the words of Scripture back to the One who breathed them.

If you have a Bible and a few minutes set apart for Him, you have everything you need to connect His Word—and the incredible love revealed in it—to your life by praying Scripture over yourself. If you don't have a Bible, there are free apps you can download. I'd highly recommend getting a paper one, though. Having my own copy of the Bible helps me focus on God without any of the normal phone distractions.

Here's an example of praying Scripture. I'll use **Romans 8:38-39**.

> For I am convinced that neither death nor life, neither angels nor demons, neither the present nor the future, nor any powers, neither height nor depth, nor anything else in all creation, will be able to separate us from the love of God that is in **Christ Jesus our Lord.**

After reflecting on that verse for a minute, I would pray something like this: "God, nothing can separate me from You. Neither death nor life, neither angels nor demons, neither the present nor the future, nor any powers, neither height nor depth—nothing at all. Help me believe today that nothing can take me away from You and Your love."

Now you try it. Don't worry about what it sounds like. Let your words come from your heart—this is a response to God's incredible gift of love. Find **Psalm 23** in your Bible and write it here. Then pray over yourself.

→ Psalm 23:

→ Prayer:

Read **Ephesians 2:8-10**, but make it personal by adding your own name in the blanks.

For it is by grace _____ has been saved, through faith—and this is not from _____ , it is the gift of God—not by works, so that _____ can boast. For _____ is God's handiwork, created in Christ Jesus to do good works, which God prepared in advance for _____ to do.

SESSION ONE • WHO AND WHY

Part 5
takeaway:
Reflect and Hope

Let's talk about this past week. Did responding to His love for you change your priorities? Are you starting to think of Him and His love as the foundation of everything else in your life?

One of my favorite things to do is to look back at my past journals and workbooks to remind myself of all God has done and what He has taught me each step of the way. My hope is that you will take the time to pray and reflect each week about the way He's changing your heart. One day, these journal entries and notes will blow you away with all that God has done for you.

Here are some questions that will help you reflect. Choose a few to write about, or just use the space to journal about what is in your heart.

→ What did you recognize about your thoughts and feelings on days you spent more time with God versus days you didn't?

→ List three ways in which you grew closer to God this week.

27

→ How do you think your relationships will change as you begin to put God first?

→ During this study, how do you hope to grow in your relationship with God, yourself, and others?

Great work this week! Remember, His love is the love you are seeking—and He is seeking you with all of His heart, too. I'll see you in Session Two. We're going to take what we've learned about God's incredible, personal love for us into our next topic: learning how to love ourselves the way God commands us to.

Madi

SESSION TWO

CONVICTION AND CONFIDENCE

all together

Welcome to the Session Two group section! This section is designed for a group to use together. To get the most out of your discussion time, review the discussion questions in advance and **start with the questions most relevant to your group**. You don't have to push through every single question. There are suggested time limits for each activity—use a timer if you need one! Have your Bibles out and ready to reference.

hey again! (5 minutes)

Before you begin your study, read this note from Madi quietly to yourselves.

Last week, we talked about God's love for you—His deep, passionate, saving love. This week, I want you to look at yourself through the lens of His love and let that love change the way that you see yourself. Do you think of yourself as beautiful? As beloved? As enough? If you're anything like me, thinking of yourself that way can be a struggle. Criticism surfaces each time you look in the mirror. You scrutinize negative comments about you. You have a hard time placing a high value on yourself.

The instinct to look outside of yourself to know who you are is normal. But we have to make sure to go to the right source. The world is full of people who want to tell you who you are. But God, the One who knit you together in your mother's womb, the One who knows every hair on your head, and the One who has given you life has authority when it comes to your identity. Don't you want to know who He thinks you are?

If you're willing to ask Him, He'll show you His version of you—the real you.

Madi

SESSION TWO • CONVICTION AND CONFIDENCE

let's pray

Group leader, read the following prayer over your group.

God, we are so inclined to listen to the wrong voices about our identity. We often take our thirst for love, acceptance, security, and belonging to the wrong things, leaving us confused, conflicted, compromising who we are, and comparing what we have to others. So today we come before You asking to know more about ourselves. Help us to hunger and thirst for You and find our belonging, confidence, and identity in You. Help us throw off the lies and skewed perspectives we have of ourselves and receive the truth of who You say we are. Inspire our hearts, Father. Help us to walk in our true identity—the identity You've given us.

Because of Your love, we can love ourselves. Show us how.

amen

press play

Session Two: Conviction and Confidence
(22 minutes)

As you watch the Session Two video, use the space below to write down thoughts, quotes, and questions.

video notes

→ We need to center our identity on the love Christ has shown us.

→ When Peter learned whose he was, he learned who He was.

→ I started praying, "Lord, show me who I am in You."

→ I went from seeking man's approval to fearing God.

→ When our eyes are kept on Jesus and His truth, only then can we walk in our true identity.

→ I am already known, accepted, and loved.

talk it out (20 minutes)

Group leader, ask the group these questions and work through them together.

1. In the video, Madi asked us three questions: Who am I right now? Who do I want to be? Who does God say that I am? Take a moment to reflect, and then take turns answering those questions.

2. **Hebrews 6:19** says, "We have this hope as an anchor for the soul, firm and secure." Christ is the only thing that can anchor our souls, but we're tempted to look elsewhere for security. What (or who) else have you tried to use as an anchor? How has that worked out?

3. Choose a volunteer to read **2 Corinthians 5:15-17**. Paul writes that for anyone in Christ, "The old has gone, the new is here!" Given last week's teaching that God's love is our foundation and His love for us grounds us and is where our love comes from, what are some "old" ways of thinking about yourself? Use specific words and phrases. Inspired by the love of Christ, what are some "new" ways of thinking about yourself?

SESSION TWO • CONVICTION AND CONFIDENCE

picture this

Don't Miss This Chance! (15 minutes)

Group leader, read this note from Madi to everyone.

The Gospels reveal Christ to us, and as we long and search for the love everybody wants, there is no greater place to look than to Jesus' love! Try to picture yourself in this story. Jesus asked an important question about His identity—Peter's answer to this question revealed his heart and his identity in Christ. Jesus has the same question for you. If you were there, walking with Jesus, how would you respond to Him?

Group leader, read this week's gospel passage aloud.

Matthew 16:13–19

When Jesus came to the region of Caesarea Philippi, he asked his disciples, "Who do people say the Son of Man is?"

They replied, "Some say John the Baptist; others say Elijah; and still others, Jeremiah or one of the prophets."

"But what about you?" he asked. "Who do you say I am?"

Simon Peter answered, "You are the Messiah, the Son of the living God."

Jesus replied, "Blessed are you, Simon son of Jonah, for this was not revealed to you by flesh and blood, but by my Father in heaven. And I tell you that you are Peter, and on this rock I will build my church, and the gates of Hades will not overcome it. I will give you the keys of the kingdom of heaven; whatever you bind on earth will be bound in heaven, and whatever you loose on earth will be loosed in heaven."

Reflect on this passage using the following prompts. If you have time, discuss these questions together. You could break into groups and share, or just write them down individually.

When Jesus says "the Son of Man," He's referring to Himself.

→ What do the people around you say about Jesus? Who do *you* say He is? Are there obstacles to claiming Jesus as your Lord and Savior?

→ How did you feel when Jesus asked the question, "Who do you say I am?"

☐ hesitant ☐ confused

☐ confident ☐ other _____

→ How did Jesus reply to Peter's answer? How do you feel He would respond to yours? Is there anything you are feeling compelled to change or act on about your answer?

until next time (5 minutes)

This week, make some time to pray for one another. Have everyone write down their names on slips of paper. Pass one name out to each member of the study. Pray for the name you received, but don't tell them you're praying for them. There is great confidence in knowing there is someone praying for you by name every day, and there is great purpose in carrying the responsibility to be that for someone else. One beautiful thing about God is that He knows what each of us needs. We don't have to know all the details of each other's needs to pray for them to be met by the One who knows. It is a great experience of faith and trust to ask God for another's needs and a great blessing if you come to hear of an answered prayer.

Write the name you received here:

_____

When's the next meeting?

_____

Group leader, close your time with the following prayer.

Jesus, You call us each by name. You are the anchor for our souls—no one can offer us the security and purpose that are freely given to us by Your love. You know us fully, accept us as we are, and love us always. We get distracted by this world. We forget, and we look to the flawed people around us for acceptance and love. We often lose ourselves and who You created us to be as we chase after other people's approval, when all along You approved of us. Forgive us, Lord, and help us to look to You for everything we need and desire. We declare with conviction, "You are the Messiah, the Son of the living God." Our identity is sourced in Your identity. When we know who You are, we know who we are, and we know that we are infinitely loved.

In Jesus' name,

SESSION TWO • CONVICTION AND CONFIDENCE

ON YOUR OWN

Part 1

checking in

Week two! Let's do this.

I want you to continue prioritizing time with God. Track the time if that's helpful. Consistency is more important than length. When you make time for God, you're effectively answering His question, "Who do you say that I am?" Your answer is this: "You are more important to me than anyone else." We always make time for those we consider important.

When you make time to listen to Him, you start hearing what He has to say about you. Think about how much you know about your best friend. A lot. More than you know about other people. Why do you think that is? It's because you spend more time with her or him *and* because when you spend time together, you are fully invested, you are present, and you care about your friend. This is the relationship Jesus wants with us. This is the relationship we enter into when we choose to spend time with Him first and fully.

As you work through this personal study, **remember that it's not about filling in all the blanks. Spend time on the sections that resonate with you.** This week, we're talking about how you can know who you are—not just who you think you are, but your real identity in Christ. What pieces of evidence do you use to understand your identity—your looks, your passions, your accomplishments, the thoughts and opinions of your friends? Write a few of those down right now.

_____

_____

_____

_____

_____

_____

_____

_____

_____

I tried to find my identity in so many different things: success in sports, the attention of some boyfriend, the opinions of others—both good and bad, but the bad things were the ones that seemed to stick in my head the most. It often built up to: "Madi, you aren't good enough—not athletic enough, not pretty enough, just unworthy." When I finally started looking to Jesus to find who I really am, my understanding of what was enough changed. I started to understand that I was good enough because *He* was good enough. If I am made in God's image and I am called His daughter and Jesus is King, then my identity needs to align with that, not what my culture or school or work or social media or magazines want to call me. I need to stand up tall in the names God gives me and learn how to "be" who *He* says I am. It's time for us to stop believing and settling for the lies the world sells us and to start receiving the truth God's Word claims over us.

Invite Him to speak to you and to make some things clear this week with this prayer:

God, please send Your Holy Spirit to guide me during this
time of prayer and study. Help me to understand who
You say I am and how that is different from what the world says.
Jesus said to love others as I love myself—help me to
understand what that means and teach me how
to love myself all for Your glory, not my own.

I want to revisit a few questions I asked you during the group session. Have you ever felt like:

→ **You were too much?**

☐ all the time ☐ sometimes ☐ never

→ **You weren't enough?**

☐ all the time ☐ sometimes ☐ never

→ **You were unworthy?**

☐ all the time ☐ sometimes ☐ never

→ **You were unlovable?**

☐ all the time ☐ sometimes ☐ never

Write out any other lies and labels you've been believing about yourself.

_____
_____
_____
_____
_____
_____

I have wrestled with these feelings, too. And I have something to say to both of us: We're not the ultimate authority about our identities. **You are more than the way you feel about yourself.** Who are you? You are who God says you are. Look up the following verses. Use these verses to inspire some different words and phrases that accurately describe who you are—that is, who God says you are. Knowing who you are starts with knowing who He is and what He says about you.

Genesis 1:27

I am . . .

_____
_____
_____
_____
_____

1 Thessalonians 1:4

I am . . .

_____
_____
_____
_____
_____

Ephesians 1:7

I am . . .

_____
_____
_____
_____
_____

1 Peter 2:9

I am . . .

_____
_____
_____
_____

Matthew 5:14

I am . . .

_____
_____
_____
_____

Romans 8:37

I am . . .

_____
_____
_____
_____

Philippians 3:20

I am . . .

_____
_____
_____
_____
_____

This week, focus on who *He* says you are.

My prayer for you this week is that
through time with Him, you will discover
that your identity is rooted in His.

THE LOVE EVERYBODY WANTS

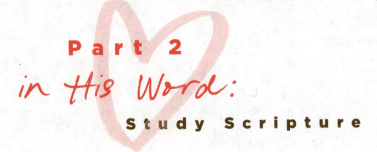

Part 2
in His Word:
Study Scripture

Let's read another gospel passage together: **John 4:7-30**

I love this story—Jesus meets a woman exactly where she is, but it didn't end there. At first, she has plenty of questions about who this man is—but watch throughout this story how her posture and confidence change as she discovers just who it is that she is talking to.

When a Samaritan woman came to draw water, Jesus said to her, "Will you give me a drink?" (His disciples had gone into the town to buy food.)

The Samaritan woman said to him, "You are a Jew and I am a Samaritan woman. How can you ask me for a drink?" (For Jews do not associate with Samaritans.)

Jesus answered her, "If you knew the gift of God and who it is that asks you for a drink, you would have asked him and he would have given you living water."

"Sir," the woman said, "you have nothing to draw with and the well is deep. Where can you get this living water? Are you greater than our father Jacob, who gave us the well and drank from it himself, as did also his sons and his livestock?"

Jesus answered, "Everyone who drinks this water will be thirsty again, but whoever drinks the water I give them will never thirst. Indeed, the water I give them will become in them a spring of water welling up to eternal life."

The woman said to him, "Sir, give me this water so that I won't get thirsty and have to keep coming here to draw water."

He told her, "Go, call your husband and come back."

"I have no husband," she replied.

Jesus said to her, "You are right when you say you have no husband. The fact is, you have had five husbands, and the man you now have is not your husband. What you have just said is quite true."

"Sir," the woman said, "I can see that you are a prophet. Our ancestors worshiped on this mountain, but you Jews claim that the place where we must worship is in Jerusalem."

"Woman," Jesus replied, "believe me, a time is coming when you will worship the Father neither on this mountain nor in Jerusalem. You Samaritans worship what you do not know; we worship what we do know, for salvation is from the Jews. Yet a time is coming and has now come when the true worshipers will worship the Father in the Spirit and in truth, for they are the kind of worshipers the Father seeks. God is spirit, and his worshipers must worship in the Spirit and in truth."

The woman said, "I know that Messiah" (called Christ) "is coming. When he comes, he will explain everything to us."

Then Jesus declared, "I, the one speaking to you—I am he."

Just then his disciples returned and were surprised to find him talking with a woman. But no one asked, "What do you want?" or "Why are you talking with her?"

> **Then, leaving her water jar, the woman went back to the town and said to the people, "Come, see a man who told me everything I ever did. Could this be the Messiah?" They came out of the town and made their way toward him.**

→ What do you feel when you read that passage? How can you relate to the woman at the well?

→ What have you been running to or thirsting after, hoping it would satisfy the longings of your heart?

- ☐ accomplishments
- ☐ relationships
- ☐ other people's approval
- ☐ success and significance
- ☐ other _____

Jesus met the woman at the well exactly where she was. But He loved her too much to just let her go and remain as she was. He called her out of her sin in a loving and truth-filled way. He knew there was more for her life. He knew that sin was creating shame in her life. He called her out not to humiliate her, but to free her. The truth sets people free!

→ What sin in your life right now has created shame and kept you from feeling loved by God and handicapped your ability to love yourself? Jot down what Jesus' sacrifice of His life *for you* actually means. He thought you were worth it—do you agree?

Part 3
weekly challenge:
Share Your Testimony

> Always be prepared to give an answer to everyone who asks you to give the reason for the hope that you have. But do this with gentleness and respect.
>
> **1 Peter 3:15**

The woman at the well was the first person Jesus revealed Himself to as the Messiah. It wasn't Peter, James, or John. It wasn't a religious teacher. It was this woman at the well. Who is unnamed in Scripture. Who is living a life of sin. Who is an outcast. He looks at her after she expresses her hope for the Messiah who is to come, and He tells her, "I, the one speaking to you—I am he."

If Jesus chose the woman at the well with the greatest news of all time, why wouldn't He choose you, too?

This week, I want you to be like the woman at the well. After she hears Jesus say that He's the Messiah, she leaves her water jug at the well and runs back to her town. She abandons the very reason she was there in the first place and runs and tells everyone she sees about this man she met at the well.

→ What do you need to let go of in order to live out who God has called and created you to be? What lies and entanglements do you need to leave behind to walk in your God-given identity?

She began boasting in the very things that had her bound for so long. The very things that might have caused isolation and anxiety in her life became her testimony and a testament to God's power.

→ Could your freedom lead to someone else's freedom? Could your confidence and love for yourself lead to someone else's?

Share your testimony or story with someone, even the hard parts. Watch as it brings you confidence, freedom, and purpose and gives glory to God.

Write out your testimony here. Find someone this week to share it with. It can be a stranger. A friend. A family member. Just start sharing it!

My hope is that as you think about, write out, and share your testimony with others about all that Jesus has given you and rescued you from, you will begin to experience true freedom and purpose.

SESSION TWO • CONVICTION AND CONFIDENCE

Part 4
to His heart:
Prayer and Worship

When we read God's words, we understand more of who He is and who we are in Him. Taking these verses to prayer will help you receive and believe the truth that your identity is rooted in His unchanging love.

→ Look up **2 Corinthians 5:17** and write it here. Pray the words of this verse over yourself.

→ Do we believe that our past defines us or that the finished work of Jesus defines us? Do we believe that culture—which is constantly shifting and changing—defines us or that the Word of God that is never changing or failing defines us?

→ Look up **Matthew 5:6** and write it out.

→ You were created to thirst, but to thirst for Him. You were created to crave, but to only be filled and satisfied by Him. Nothing else this world offers will fulfill you. Only Jesus can. Write a prayer asking Him to satisfy your thirst.

→ Look up **1 Peter 2:9** and **Psalm 139:16**. Pray these verses over the name you drew during the group study time.

SESSION TWO • CONVICTION AND CONFIDENCE

Part 5
takeaway:
Reflect and Hope

How did this week go? Look back at your calendar. Are your thoughts about yourself starting to change?

I try to remember my old self with compassion—old Madi made mistakes and she had weird ideas about what was important, but God really loved her. God's love for me was kind, and patient, and enduring. Over time, I learned to prioritize what He said about me over everything else. I learned to answer the question, "Who do you say that I am?" I learned to ask Jesus to give me what I needed. My identity is caught up in Him—I can love myself because of His great love for me.

Here are some questions and prompts to help you reflect. Choose a few to write about, or just use the space to journal about what is in your heart.

→ Has your perspective on your identity changed at all this week? How?

→ List some negative thoughts you've had about yourself—feel free to cross them out after you write them!

55

→ Write a declaration statement about your true God-given identity. This will be helpful to write on a sticky note and put on your mirror to serve as a reminder of who you are even when your feelings or the Enemy disagrees.

→ What truth about your identity did you learn this week? Write down anything in this study or from Scripture that stood out to you and helped you this week view yourself the way Jesus views you.

_____
_____
_____
_____
_____
_____
_____

Great work this week! Your identity is tied up in His—this is great news, because He is loving and good! I'll see you in Session Three. We're going to take what we've learned about our identity in Christ to our mission in this world: loving others as we love ourselves.

Madi

SESSION THREE

PATTERNS, PURPOSE, AND PEACE

all together

Welcome to the Session Three group section! This section is designed for a group to use together. To get the most out of your discussion time, review the discussion questions in advance and **start with the questions most relevant to your group**. You don't have to push through every single question. There are suggested time limits for each activity—use a timer if you need one! Have your Bibles out and ready to reference.

hey again! (5 minutes)

Before you begin your study, read this note from Madi quietly to yourselves.

In the past two sessions, we learned about God's love for us and how we can love ourselves in light of that love. We're finally ready to talk about what it looks like to love others well. It's tempting to do this backward— we go searching for the love everybody wants in our relationships with others first. But we can only love others well if we already know that we're loved.

We can offer God's love to others, but we can't find it in them.

When we are rooted in God's love and confident in our identity in Christ, we aren't looking to anyone else to complete us or tell us who we are. We stop asking for the things that our families, friends, and significant others just can't give us.

Madi

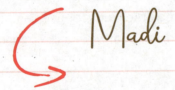

SESSION THREE • PATTERNS, PURPOSE, AND PEACE

let's pray

Group leader, read the following prayer over your group.

God, we come before You asking You for the grace to love others well and to receive love humbly from others. We know that You created each one of us with joy, and You are still rejoicing over us. You freely extend to us the love that we desire—we are complete in You! We can rely on Your sacrifice. We can stop believing lies, and we can start pointing others toward You.

Our desire is to love our neighbors as You've taught us to love ourselves. Give us grace, Father, as we learn how to live out Your greatest commandment.

press play

Session Three: Patterns, Purpose, and Peace
(22 minutes)

As you watch the Session Three video, use the space below to write down thoughts, quotes, and questions.

video notes

→ The problems begin with a bad foundation.

→ We were created for relationships.

→ The three P's: Patterns, Purpose, Peace

SESSION THREE • PATTERNS, PURPOSE, AND PEACE

→ You can't build a life together on two different foundations.

→ If it's the wrong person OR the wrong time, it's the wrong love.

→ You were created for holiness.

→ Ask yourself: Will this relationship or behavior help me run my race and reach my purpose or not?

→ Look for action, not attraction.

talk it out (20 minutes)

Group leader, ask the group these questions and work through them together.

1. We were made for relationships: a relationship with God and relationships with others. But we learn through Scripture that relationships with other people matter, and they impact our relationship with God and ourselves. Who in your life is leading you away from God—what does that look like? Who in your life is leading you closer to God—how are they helping you?

2. How have you seen God in your relationships? What is the difference in your relationships when you can see Him clearly versus when you cannot?

3. Choose a volunteer to read **Hebrews 12:1–2**. Madi offers this verse as a new perspective on the question many of us wonder when it comes to boundaries and purity: "How far is too far?" After all, that's just the wrong question. Based on the concepts in this verse, what should we be striving for in our relationships with others? What boundaries do you need to set in your current relationships? Remember, setting boundaries does not make you crazy, it makes you loving.

picture this

Don't Miss This Chance! (15 minutes)

Group leader, read this note from Madi to everyone.

Let's see Jesus in this gospel passage—He extends mercy to someone who needs it desperately. Have you ever been in that position before? This one is so personal! Try to picture yourself in the story.

Once again, leaders and teachers were questioning Jesus—John goes so far as to say that these leaders were trying to trap Him. After catching a woman in sin, they drag her in front of Him and ask for His judgment—what does someone like her deserve?

Group leader, read this week's gospel passage aloud.

John 8:1-11

At dawn he appeared again in the temple courts, where all the people gathered around him, and he sat down to teach them. The teachers of the law and the Pharisees brought in a woman caught in adultery. They made her stand before the group and said to Jesus, "Teacher, this woman was caught in the act of adultery. In the Law Moses commanded us to stone such women. Now what do you say?" They were using this question as a trap, in order to have a basis for accusing him.

But Jesus bent down and started to write on the ground with his finger. When they kept on questioning him, he straightened up and said to them, "Let any one of you who is without sin be the first to throw a stone at her." Again he stooped down and wrote on the ground.

At this, those who heard began to go away one at a time, the older ones first, until only Jesus was left, with the woman still standing there. Jesus straightened up and asked her, "Woman, where are they? Has no one condemned you?"

"No one, sir," she said.

"Then neither do I condemn you," Jesus declared. "Go now and leave your life of sin."

Reflect on this passage using the following prompts. If you have time, discuss these questions out loud. You could break into groups and share, or just write them down individually.

→ Have you ever been caught doing something you shouldn't have been doing? How did you feel?

☐ ashamed ☐ angry
☐ afraid   ☐ indifferent

→ How does Jesus respond to the teachers and Pharisees? How does He respond to the woman?

→ Imagine that you are the woman caught in sin. What would be your response to Jesus' words: "Then neither do I condemn you . . . Go now and leave your life of sin."

65

until next time (5 minutes)

This week, meet up with some of the members of your group to pray together. In **Matthew 18:20**, Jesus says, "'For where two or three gather in my name, there am I with them.'" This doesn't have to be a long gathering or a large one. Jesus just said "two or three"! So try it. Once this week, schedule half an hour of in-person prayer time before work or school. You could meet at a coffee shop, someone's house, or at a park. As you pray for each other, remember what Jesus said to you: "There am I with them." What an amazing promise!

When's the next meeting?

Group leader, close your time with the following prayer.

Jesus, You spent Your life on earth loving others,
and You're giving us the same incredible opportunity.
Known by Your Father and confident in Your identity,
You looked on others with forgiveness. You drew
them away from sin and toward God. There are so many
sins that easily entangle us, but in Your mercy, we can
leave that life of sin behind. We can see
Your purpose in all of our relationships and all
of the seasons we experience. Through everything,
You've given us Your love—we can only
give others what we've first received from You.
In everything, we want to
love others as we love ourselves.

In Jesus' name,

ON YOUR OWN

Part 1

checking in

You've made it to week three. Did you think it would be this long before we actually started diving into your relationships with others? Maybe not! Well, I hope you've been able to tap into the reasons for the wait. There's no worthy substitute for a firm foundation—we need to know we're loved and to love ourselves before we can love anyone else well. As Christ commanded us in **John 13:34–35**, "A new command I give you: Love one another. As I have loved you, so you must love one another. By this everyone will know that you are my disciples, if you love one another."

So let's do it. **As you work through these questions, remember that you don't have to get through everything just to fill in the blanks.** Spend time on the questions that really challenge you. Let's talk about your relationships with others. Can someone tell that you follow Jesus just by the way you treat others, including in your romantic relationships? Why or why not?

Maybe you look at your life and find the evidence is a little mixed—sometimes you're loving and sacrificial, and sometimes you aren't! You're not the only one. I was reading this verse one day and was so convicted. Everyone will know if I follow Jesus or not, just by the way I treat others. It really convicted me to pay more attention to how I treat others: how I talk to them, about them, view them, pray for them. No one loves others perfectly—no one except for Jesus. We all need grace, and we all need forgiveness. One of the ways we can start loving others well is by acknowledging the ways we've messed up in the past—the ways we don't want to repeat in the future.

As you ask Him to show you how to love others, invite His Holy Spirit into this work with this prayer:

God, please send Your Holy Spirit to guide me during this time of prayer and study. Jesus commanded me to love others— through the grace You've extended to me, help me to love others.

On a scale of one to ten, if one is "Not at all" and ten is "Definitely," would you say that you love others well?

We are called to love others God's way, not our way—even the others we are in dating relationships with. If you're not dating or in this season of life right now, this still applies to the "others" you are in relationship and friendship with. I said this in the video, too, but I want to say it again: I was not perfect in my dating relationships. I have made some bad decisions, and I have broken boundaries. I have learned a lot since then about how important boundaries are and what it means to truly love my neighbor. Whatever it is that you are struggling with, please know this: God loves you and wants to untangle you from all of it. I know that God redeems my sins—He gave me the grace to acknowledge my missteps and to try again. I kept coming back to Him, the source of the love that I really wanted, and I found the grace to try again, the guidance how to, and the encouragement that I wasn't stuck in my bad choices.

Don't you want to experience that freedom?

Establishing your boundaries before you start dating and declaring your boundaries in dating are some of the most loving things you can do. Living by the standard of truth that God has called us to is one of the best ways to love ourselves and our neighbors. Culture, even church, can tend to go to the extremes—either "Sex is bad, don't even think about it!" or "Sex isn't a big deal at all!" —but neither of those ideas expresses the truth.

The truth is that sex is a beautiful and good gift, but it is only loving in the context of marriage. Not out of shame or fear, but with an understanding of the truth and the desire to love my neighbor, I decided to save myself for marriage. I came up with standards that I held myself accountable to through confession to my friends—I confessed (and still do confess!) these sins, even if they are "just" thoughts.

Use these questions to start thinking through your own standards:

→ **What kinds of impure thoughts have I indulged in? What could I think about instead?**

I DON'T WANT TO THINK ABOUT . . .	I DO WANT TO THINK ABOUT . . .

→ **What have I looked at that I shouldn't have looked at? What do I want to fix my eyes on instead?**

I DON'T WANT TO LOOK AT . . .	I DO WANT TO LOOK AT . . .

THE LOVE EVERYBODY WANTS

→ What have I done in dating relationships that I now regret, or what kinds of actions do I want to avoid completely during the season of dating? What actions are truly loving toward someone I'm dating?

UNLOVING ACTIONS	LOVING ACTIONS

My prayer for you this week is that the love you've felt from God will overflow into your relationships with others.

SESSION THREE • PATTERNS, PURPOSE, AND PEACE

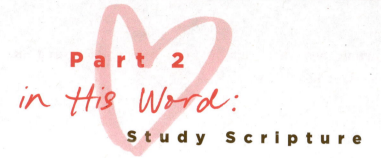

Part 2
in His Word: Study Scripture

Let's read this passage together: **1 Corinthians 13:4–13**

Scripture is the ultimate standard of how we should love others. If you're trying to love others without drawing from the love that God has for you, you'll find yourself burnt out and defeated. In **1 Corinthians 13**, Paul writes about Christian love—love sourced in God never fails.

Use a pen, pencil, or highlighter to interact with the text. Find the same passage in your own Bible.

> Love is patient, love is kind. It does not envy, it does not boast, it is not proud. It does not dishonor others, it is not self-seeking, it is not easily angered, it keeps no record of wrongs. Love does not delight in evil but rejoices with the truth. It always protects, always trusts, always hopes, always perseveres.
>
> Love never fails. But where there are prophecies, they will cease; where there are tongues, they will be stilled; where there is knowledge, it will pass away. For we know in part and we prophesy in part, but when completeness comes, what is in part disappears. When I was a child, I talked like a child, I thought like a child, I reasoned like a child. When I became a man, I put the ways of childhood behind me. For now we see only a reflection as in a mirror; then we shall see face to face. Now I know in part; then I shall know fully, even as I am fully known.

And now these three remain: faith, hope and love. But the greatest of these is love.

→ Verse 4 begins with "Love is patient." Write out that paragraph below, replacing "love" and "it" with your own name.

→ Do you live up to this version of love? What in your life would need to change for this paragraph to be recognizable as you? What aspect of love do you struggle with the most? Do you struggle with patience, or anger, or "keeping score"?

→ How is your love for others different when you're loving them out of the overflow of God's love for you?

SESSION THREE • PATTERNS, PURPOSE, AND PEACE

Part 3
weekly challenge:
Confess Your Sins

> Therefore confess your sins to each other and pray for each other so that you may be healed.
>
> **James 5:16**

"Confess" is a word that means "make known" or "acknowledge." When we make our sins known, we give others the chance to pray for us and for our healing. Have you ever shared your struggles with someone that you trusted would keep them completely confidential?

We can find healing from the sin in our lives, but we have to first bring it out of the darkness. This can be scary, but it brings so much freedom. This week, I want you to try confessing your sins to someone who is also seeking Christ—someone you trust. I've incorporated this practice into my life, and it is both humbling and fruitful. Confessing my sins actually helps me stay away from sin, and it also gives my friends an amazing, practical way to love me.

Here's how I'd go about confessing:

Ask the Holy Spirit to convict you—don't leave out any sins that the Holy Spirit brings to your mind. Write down what you need to confess.

THE LOVE EVERYBODY WANTS

Prayerfully choose someone you trust (choose someone who is your same gender)—the person to whom you confess should be someone who follows Christ in word and actions *and* who can resist the temptation to gossip. If you do not know someone who fits this standard, pray for God to bring a person of this standard into your life.

Ask this person if they will hear your confession—this can be kind of awkward, but you don't want to just drop this in the middle of a conversation without letting them prepare. You can also offer to hear their confession, too. I like to ask it like this: "Can I confess something to you?"

Confess your sins with sincerity and without excuses—own your actions. Then, ask your friend to pray over you—using words from their heart or from Scripture, such as **1 John 1:9**: "If we confess our sins, he is faithful and just and will forgive us our sins and purify us from all unrighteousness."

→ What did you feel after you confessed? Was it what you expected?

My hope is that confessing your sins will help you understand that you are *forgiven by God*. Only in forgiveness and freedom can your relationships be all they were created to be.

SESSION THREE • PATTERNS, PURPOSE, AND PEACE

Part 4
to His heart:
Prayer and Worship

It can feel impossible to hold yourself to God's standard for loving others. Lean on Scripture. Speak these verses aloud when you find yourself tempted to do something that isn't loving toward your neighbor.

→ Look up **Hebrews 12:1-2** and write it here.

→ Notice the actions required in order for us to keep our eyes fixed on Jesus and to run the race He has for us well. How do you feel these two verses contradict the natural temptation of asking "How far is too far?" What is God calling you to do?

→ What kinds of actions indulge the flesh—purely selfish, just to feel good? What kinds of actions constitute service for others? Think of a few examples of selfish actions, and write them in the left column in the chart. On the right side, list actions that qualify as loving others in service.

INDULGING THE FLESH	SERVING ONE ANOTHER

→ Pray for the freedom to serve one another instead of giving in to selfishness. If you're in a relationship, pray for this kind of freedom for yourself and for them.

→ Read **Psalm 51:10-12**.

> Create in me a pure heart, O God,
>> and renew a steadfast spirit within me.
>
> Do not cast me from your presence
>> or take your Holy Spirit from me.
>
> Restore to me the joy of your salvation
>> and grant me a willing spirit, to sustain me.

God forgives all sins. Sometimes, we relegate sexual sins to this different category, forgetting that He extends mercy over everything. King David wrote this psalm after falling into terrible sins (sexual sins included!). Nothing you've done—or ever will do—is beyond His forgiveness.

Part 5
takeaway:
Reflect and Hope

In the group session, I told a story about a house I once lived in with a roommate. Everything looked good on the surface—it was renovated and updated and, at first glance, I loved it. But there was a big problem. The foundation was uneven, so all of those beautiful updates were ruined. That's because you can't build a strong and lasting house on a bad foundation. The way you love others is totally dependent on your foundation. It all starts with believing that God loves you and that His love for you is enough. You don't *need* anyone else. Because of His sacrifice, you are enough, too—His great love for you allows you to love yourself. With your foundation intact, you can love others without fear, without judgment, without comparison, or need for reciprocation. You can stop falling into sin with them. You can ask God honestly, "What does that person need today to know that they are loved?" You can seek His will, asking Him, "How can I love the person I'm dating in the ways that You would want me to love them?"

We need our own strong foundation, but we also need to surround ourselves with other people whose foundations are strong. Are there others around you who are trying to live out the greatest commandment, or are you the only one? **Matthew 7:24** says, "Therefore everyone who hears these words of mine and puts them into practice is like a wise man who built his house on the rock." Before you get into a relationship with anyone, ask yourself, "What is this person's foundation?" If they aren't building on rock, they're going to crumble under pressure.

Here are some questions and prompts that will help you reflect. Choose a few to write about, or just use the space to journal about what is in your heart.

Before I met my husband, I started considering every potential relationship with my three P's—Patterns, Purpose, and Peace. It's so important to know what you're looking for. I always encourage my friends, "Keep your standards high and roots deep." When we are rooted in truth, it brings clarity to our lives and relationships, giving us vision and direction. Let God's Word and love guide your standards. Make your own version of the three P's and write them down.

→ Did this study bring up ways to love others that you hadn't thought about before? What are they? Take some time to write out how you are going to put this new perspective into practice, so you claim your behavior before you live it out.

Bad company corrupts good character. And good company grows good character! The Bible says if you want to be wise, surround yourself with wise people. Your friends will either push you toward Jesus and freedom, or they will push you further away from Jesus and into shame.

→ Are your relationships helping you walk in your purpose and make a difference for Jesus?

→ **What is a small change that you could make in your own relationships that would help you and others prioritize Christ?**

Remember, setting boundaries is loving. Write a draft of a purity contract and send it to one of your friends for accountability.

Loving others is no easy task, but God has called us to the greatest possible mission—sharing in His love for every single one of His children. We are so blessed to be His and to be a part of this! I'll see you in Session Four. We've walked through each part of Jesus' greatest commandment: Love God. Love yourself. Love others. Next week, we'll talk about submitting our entire lives to this commandment. We'll learn why God's way is just better.

SESSION FOUR

STAND FIRM AND SURRENDER

all together

Welcome to the Session Four group section! This section is designed for a group to use together. To get the most out of your discussion time, review the discussion questions in advance and **start with the questions most relevant to your group**. You don't have to push through every single question. There are suggested time limits for each activity—use a timer if you need one! Have your Bibles out and ready to reference.

hey again! (5 minutes)

Before you begin your study, read this note from Madi quietly to yourselves.

You are already loved in the ways you've been longing for. God created you lovingly, fulfills you completely, and equips you to love others faithfully. The right response to the greatest commandment—love God, love yourself, love others—is surrender. Surrender is letting go of control. It's choosing to follow God instead of following your own desires.

During this study, you've had the chance to dig into Scripture, make time for prayer, and seek godly community. Through these practices, have you started to see how God's way is better than your own way? You want the world to see your accomplishments, but God says that you'll only be fulfilled when you seek Him first. You long to find and build your own identity, but God says you were made in His image—His child—created in Him to do good works in His name. You hunger and thirst for significance and belonging around you, but God says only in Him will you be filled. You set your hope in yourself and take your life into your own

SESSION FOUR • STAND FIRM AND SURRENDER

hands, but God says those who find their lives only lose them, and only in surrendering to Him will you find it.

What is He asking you to surrender?

You'll never regret giving Him control. God will not only bless your surrender, but He will use it to bless others, too.

Madi

let's pray

Group leader, read the following prayer over your group.

God, we want to surrender to You fully. Our hearts have come up with so many plans, and many of those plans don't have You at the center. Help us to release those plans back to You now. Scripture reminds us that Your ways and thoughts are higher and better than ours. You are so patient with us, and You continue to offer us the love that we want—not the love that we've planned for, not the love that we would design for ourselves, but the love given freely in the sacrifice of Your Son, who surrendered fully to You.

Created with love, complete in Christ, and surrounded by godly community, we want to surrender our lives in service to You. Father, give us the strength to surrender.

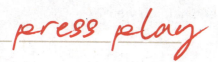

Session Four: Stand Firm and Surrender
(21 minutes)

As you watch the Session Four video, use the space below to write down thoughts, quotes, and questions.

video notes

→ God's love is always worth it.

→ Who are we to think we know better than God?

→ Sarah takes control **(Genesis 16)**.

→ What happens when you don't get what you want?

→ Surrender is giving up all control to God.

→ Surrender is never easy, but it is worth it.

→ Our way is darkness, but God's way is light.

→ We are made for love.

SESSION FOUR • STAND FIRM AND SURRENDER

talk it out (20 minutes)

Group leader, ask the group these questions and work through them together.

1. In the video, Madi told the story of Isaac's conception **(Genesis 16, 21)**. God's promise to Sarah and Abraham—the promise of a son in their very old age—didn't make sense. It didn't even seem possible. Is there anything in your life you feel God is calling you to that feels impossible? Do you trust that God knows best even when you don't understand?

2. **Genesis 21:1** says, "Now the Lord was gracious to Sarah as he had said, and the Lord did for Sarah what he had promised." Even though Sarah tried to control her life, God was still faithful to her. How has God been faithful to you, even when you doubted that He would do what He promised?

3. Surrender not only leads you closer to God, but it leads you closer to your purpose here on this earth. We were made to make a difference and we do that by serving others. Surrender leads to service. How does surrendering to His will prepare you for service to others? When you focus on service, how does your perspective about relationships change?

picture this

Don't Miss This Chance! (15 minutes)

Group leader, read this note from Madi to everyone.

The perfect model of surrender is Jesus Himself. Even for Him, it wasn't easy! Just before He offered His life for yours, He struggled with His Father. As Jesus cried and prayed in the garden of Gethsemane, His heart was prepared for the perfect act of surrender.

Sometimes what comes with surrender is not blessing, success, and happiness. Sometimes what comes out of surrender is suffering. That may sound scary to you—no one wants to suffer. But I have learned suffering from sin is much worse than suffering through something God has called me into that will lead me closer to His best for me. Jesus experienced what it is to suffer now for an eventual better. This passage tells us about the worst night of Jesus' life—He was torn, and alone, and overwhelmed. He knew that He was going to suffer a painful death. He asked His Father if there was another way. But He didn't cave in—He surrendered to God's will.

Group leader, read this week's gospel passage aloud.

Matthew 26:36–46

Then Jesus went with his disciples to a place called Gethsemane, and he said to them, "Sit here while I go over there and pray." He took Peter and the two sons of Zebedee along with him, and he began to be sorrowful and troubled. Then he said to them, "My soul is overwhelmed with sorrow to the point of death. Stay here and keep watch with me."

Going a little farther, he fell with his face to the ground and prayed, "My Father, if it is possible, may this cup be taken from me. Yet not as I will, but as you will."

Then he returned to his disciples and found them sleeping. "Couldn't you men keep watch with me for one hour?" he asked Peter. "Watch and pray so that you will not fall into temptation. The spirit is willing, but the flesh is weak."

He went away a second time and prayed, "My Father, if it is not possible for this cup to be taken away unless I drink it, may your will be done."

When he came back, he again found them sleeping, because their eyes were heavy. So he left them and went away once more and prayed the third time, saying the same thing.

Then he returned to the disciples and said to them, "Are you still sleeping and resting? Look, the hour has come, and the Son of Man is delivered into the hands of sinners. Rise! Let us go! Here comes my betrayer!"

Reflect on this passage using the following prompts. If you have time, discuss these questions out loud. You could break into groups and share, or just write them down individually.

→ **What have your times of crying out to God to keep you from having to go through something looked like or felt like?**

- ☐ tears
- ☐ fear
- ☐ stubbornness
- ☐ faith

→ What do you think of Jesus' phrase, "My soul is overwhelmed with sorrow to the point of death." Jesus can empathize with your own experiences of overwhelm and sorrow—He felt that way, too. But He was able to accept God's will for His life because He knew that it would bring salvation to others. He persevered because there was good on the other side of the darkness. Imagine Him comforting you about the difficulties you're facing. What do you feel He wants to say to you right now?

→ Where in your life do you need to say to God, "Not as I will, but as You will"? Ask God for the strength to surrender to His best in your life and relationships.

until next time (5 minutes)

Surrender leads to service. Only in surrender can we live in the fullness of who God has called us to be: His hands and feet, His servant. Jesus' surrender led to our salvation—the greatest service ever given! **What if other people's salvation and freedom were attached to your willingness to surrender?**

Spend some time brainstorming together about the needs in your community, both big and small. There are no bad ideas here. Opportunities to serve are everywhere, from your local church to your friend going through a hard time to charitable organizations to elderly relatives to the young family living down the street. This can also be a group effort—think of ways that your group could serve your community together.

Where could you go and serve? What could your surrender do for others?

Take a moment to pray over these ideas, asking God to lead you.

Group leader, close your time with the following prayer.

Jesus, even You struggled to surrender. You asked God for a different way, but in the end, You accepted His way. That night in the garden, You followed the greatest commandment—out of God's love for You and Your confidence in Him, You extended salvation to all people. We want to be like You in every way—we want to live as beloved children, free from sin and surrendered to the will of God. Out of that great love, the love everybody wants, we want to go into the world and love others.

In Jesus' name,

amen

ON YOUR OWN

Part 1

checking in

Hey—it's Madi. I can't believe that this is our last personal study together. I'm so grateful for this chance we've had to grow in our faith and love together through prayer, challenges, Scripture, and reflection. **Don't rush to get through every single question**. Please know that I'm praying for you—I've been praying for you this whole time, and no matter what your past has looked like when it comes to relationships, I believe when you surrender to God's will, the best is truly yet to come.

Surrender can be so painful. Letting go of our wants, dreams, expectations, and relationships, and trusting it all to God when we cannot see the outcome is no easy task. It forces something out of our hands that we so desperately want to control. When we surrender—when we let God take the control, no matter how much we want it—we're telling God, "I believe that You know best." We need to give God the final say in our lives because He actually does know best. Think of the good that God created out of Jesus' surrender on the cross. God will use our trust in Him for good, too!

And I can't say that for me it necessarily gets "easier" to resist the temptation to follow *my* way, but I will say over the years as I follow *His* way, I continue to see why God's way is *the* way that leads to a full life, because it is best and blessed. God has so patiently worked through my stubbornness and my desire for control. There were years where I couldn't see what He was doing, but I kept trying to say, "Your will, not my will." Even through my failures, He led me to where I am today. And you know what? I am so glad that things didn't work out according to what I thought was best, because God's best is so much better!

So, no matter where you are in your journey, I want to point you toward surrender, and to the One who surrendered perfectly. If you ask Him for help, He will show you how.

Invite the Holy Spirit into your personal study with this prayer:

God, please send Your Holy Spirit to guide me during this time of prayer. Everything I have and all that I am is Yours.

99

Let's think back to those scales that we used in the first personal study. Without looking back to the first time you did this, answer these questions using the scales below.

On a scale of one to ten, with one being terrible and ten being the absolute best . . .

How would you rate your relationship with God?

How would you rate your relationship with yourself?

Last, what about your relationships with others?

→ Now you can look back at the first section. Did your numbers change at all? Why do you think that is?

→ What has shifted in your perspective about . . .

What it means to have a relationship with God?

How accepting God's love for you helps you love yourself well?

What it means to "love your neighbor"?

How standing firm in your love for God, love for yourself, and your love for others is also an act of surrender to God?

My prayer for you this week is that He brings you to a place of surrender as you put your faith and trust in Him.

SESSION FOUR • STAND FIRM AND SURRENDER

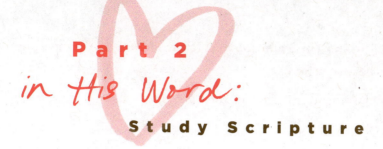

Part 2
in His Word:
Study Scripture

Let's read this gospel passage together: **John 14:1–14**

With the greatest commandment, Jesus told us that we have to follow God's way above all else. Along with the pressures and temptations that surround us in our culture, we each have our own will. We're also going to be influenced by our friends, our parents, and all of the other relationships in our lives. But amid all of those voices we can choose to surrender and listen to Jesus first.

Let's take another look at this passage that I referenced in the Session Four video. Just before Jesus was crucified, He offered words of comfort to His disciples.

"Do not let your hearts be troubled. You believe in God; believe also in me. My Father's house has many rooms; if that were not so, would I have told you that I am going there to prepare a place for you? And if I go and prepare a place for you, I will come back and take you to be with me that you also may be where I am. You know the way to the place where I am going."

Thomas said to him, "Lord, we don't know where you are going, so how can we know the way?"

Jesus answered, "I am the way and the truth and the life. No one comes to the Father except through me. If you really know me,

103

you will know my Father as well. From now on, you do know him and have seen him."

Philip said, "Lord, show us the Father and that will be enough for us."

Jesus answered: "Don't you know me, Philip, even after I have been among you such a long time? Anyone who has seen me has seen the Father. How can you say, 'Show us the Father'? Don't you believe that I am in the Father, and that the Father is in me? The words I say to you I do not speak on my own authority. Rather, it is the Father, living in me, who is doing his work. Believe me when I say that I am in the Father and the Father is in me; or at least believe on the evidence of the works themselves. Very truly I tell you, whoever believes in me will do the works I have been doing, and they will do even greater things than these, because I am going to the Father. And I will do whatever you ask in my name, so that the Father may be glorified in the Son. You may ask me for anything in my name, and I will do it.

Think about the hesitations of Thomas and Philip—Thomas said he couldn't follow Jesus because he didn't know where Jesus was going, and Philip wasn't sure about Jesus and the Father being One.

→ Consider which response you relate to more and describe your hesitation in trusting what you can't see or understand below.

→ Jesus is asking His disciples to surrender—to trust Him with everything. In this passage, what does Jesus promise to those who surrender to Him—that is, "whoever believes in me"?

→ Consider three decisions you are faced with right now, minor or major. List these decisions on the left-hand side of the chart. Think through how you want to respond to each decision and why.

DECISION	MY RESPONSE

Surrender can be a simple matter of consulting God before you act and acting on how the Holy Spirit leads you. Sit quietly with God and the decisions you listed in the chart. Ask the Holy Spirit to reveal His responses for you. Does anything about your responses change when you ask God to help you surrender?

Part 3
weekly challenge:
Serve Others

> For even the Son of Man did not come to be served, but to serve, and to give his life as a ransom for many.
>
> **Mark 10:45**

Even Jesus, the Son of God, was sent to earth to serve, and if we are to be like Jesus, that should be our mission. In our relationships with one another, **Philippians 2** challenges us to have the same mindset as Christ Jesus had. And **Matthew 25:31-46** reminds us that when we serve others, we are actually serving Jesus. **Verses 37-40** say, "Then the righteous will answer him, 'Lord, when did we see you hungry and feed you, or thirsty and give you something to drink? When did we see you a stranger and invite you in, or needing clothes and clothe you? When did we see you sick or in prison and go to visit you?' The King will reply, 'Truly I tell you, whatever you did for one of the least of these brothers and sisters of mine, you did for me.'"

We weren't saved and set free just to live a comfortable and selfish life. We were saved and set free to serve, by telling others about Jesus and being the hands and feet of Jesus. God's way is never about "me" and always about Him. God is about serving others. Jesus served everyone

He came into contact with—with truth, love, hope, purpose, freedom, joy, peace, and confidence!

When we take our eyes off of ourselves, we begin to see the needs around us and use what has been given to us to help those around us. Needs can be tangible or they can be emotional or they can be spiritual. We can provide help, friendship, or encouragement, or we can provide prayer and intercession. According to **Ephesians 4**, in order to live a life worthy of the calling we have received, we should walk in surrender and holiness, always eager to serve in love and bless those we encounter.

Write the needs you see around you in the left side of the chart. Fill in the other side with ideas about how you can serve with the gifts God has given you.

NEEDS I SEE	WHAT I COULD DO

Commit to one act of service this week. Think about ways that you could avoid getting recognition for it—what could you do behind the scenes?

Part 4
to His heart:
Prayer and Worship

It can be so hard to accept God's will. The thoughts in our minds can be relentless: "It would be so much better if . . .", "If only I had done it differently . . .", "I'd feel loved if I was in a relationship . . ." At the root of it, these kinds of thoughts are just like three-year-old us throwing a tantrum, insisting on "MY WAY!" One of the best ways to counter our straying thoughts and accept God's will is to turn to His Word. Pray these shorter pieces of Scripture over yourself and others, asking God for the grace to know that His way is the best way and for the strength to follow it.

→ Look up **Proverbs 14:12**, and fill in the blank.

There is a way that appears to be right, but in the end it leads to _____.

Think about a situation when you followed your own way instead of God's and what that led to: Shame? Rejection? Bitterness? Anger? Lust? Emptiness? Brokenness? Betrayal? Pray this proverb over yourself as a reminder that our feelings are valid but not always right. Just because you feel something, doesn't mean you should follow it. When you are faced with a decision, turn to God's Word, remember this proverb, and pray.

→ In **Proverbs 3:5–6**, circle the words of this verse that stick out to you the most.

Trust in the Lord with all your heart and lean not on your own understanding; in all your ways submit to him, and he will make your paths straight.

SESSION FOUR • STAND FIRM AND SURRENDER

→ What does God promise you when you trust in Him over yourself?

→ In **John 15:5**, Jesus speaks to you. Fill in the blank with your name.

I am the vine; _____ is the branches. If _____ remains in me and I in you, _____ will bear much fruit; apart from me you can do nothing.

What does this verse speak to you?

Not only does surrender to God lead to His presence and provision but it also leads to His protection. Surrendering and submitting to God protects us against the Enemy.

→ Look up **James 4:7** and write it below.

When you face temptation, pray for the strength to resist evil—even at the thought level. Remember the power of your surrender—the devil flees when you resist him!

THE LOVE EVERYBODY WANTS

Part 5
takeaway:
Reflect and Hope

This study has taken us through all the parts of Jesus' greatest commandment: Love God, love yourself, and love others. We don't do any of these naturally—it's part of our fallen nature to seek love that isn't God's love, to seek identity apart from God, and to entangle others in sin that is not reflective of or honoring to God. But God's way for us truly is the better and best way. By obeying the greatest commandment, we experience the love everybody wants.

Has your perspective on relationships changed over the last few weeks? Use these prompts to write about how you can see your heart changing.

→ How would you explain Jesus' greatest commandment to a friend?

→ What does it really mean to love yourself? How does what you learned during these past few weeks compare with what you've heard before?

→ Before you started this study, what did you think of as a promising romantic relationship? Has your view changed—how would you describe a promising romantic relationship now?

→ The weekly challenges—planning time with God, sharing your testimony, confessing your sins, and serving others—were ways to live out the greatest commandment. How could you incorporate the actions of these challenges into your daily life?

When life feels overwhelming and temptations and pressures arise all around you, remember and pray **John 14:6**: "Jesus answered, 'I am the way and the truth and the life. No one comes to the Father except through me.'" God's way isn't just right, it's so much better. It's not just what will get you into heaven one day. It's what gives you peace, purpose, and hope here on earth. It's what fills you and satisfies every longing and desire deep in your heart.

Jesus addresses all of our longings for love with this, His greatest commandment: "'Love the Lord your God with all your heart and with all your soul and with all your mind.' This is the first and greatest commandment. And the second is like it: 'Love your neighbor as yourself'" (**Matthew 22:37–39**).

In every relationship we find ourselves in, we must cling to these words if we want to love well.

Our entire faith is built on relationships. I pray that through this study you discovered the value in building healthy and holy relationships. God's love meets your every want and need. His love is the only one that will ever satisfy you fully and completely. Scripture says it is out of the overflow of God's love that we can love ourselves and others.

It has been such an honor to do this study with you. You are God's beloved child. He created you and knows you fully and can give you the strength you need to live a life of freedom and surrender to His will. Thank you for this chance to share my heart with you—I pray with hope that these few weeks have helped you lean into the great love that is already ours.

about the author

Madison Prewett Troutt, bestselling author of *Made for This Moment*, is a speaker and social media influencer best known as a finalist on the reality television show, "The Bachelor." Madi has a degree in communications from Auburn University and a certificate in ministry in pastoral leadership through Highlands College. She has been involved in many outreach programs, including Adullam House, Make It Matter, Autlive, and Auburn Dream Center. Madi started her career working as a foster parent recruiter in Birmingham, Alabama. She lives in Waco, Texas, with her husband, Grant.

ALSO AVAILABLE FROM MADISON PREWETT TROUTT

THE LOVE EVERYBODY WANTS

WHAT YOU'RE LOOKING FOR IS ALREADY YOURS

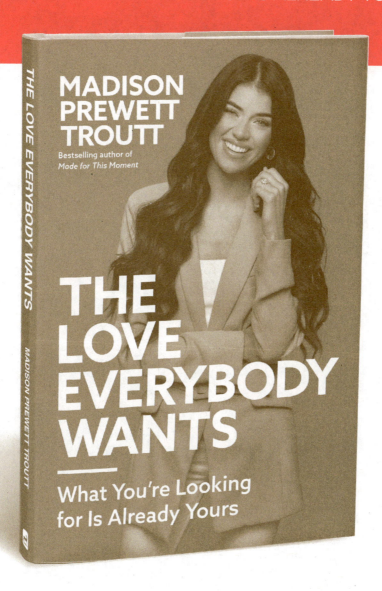

Available in stores and online!

WATERBROOK

MORE FROM MADISON PREWETT TROUTT

MADE FOR THIS MOMENT

Standing Firm with Strength, Grace, and Courage

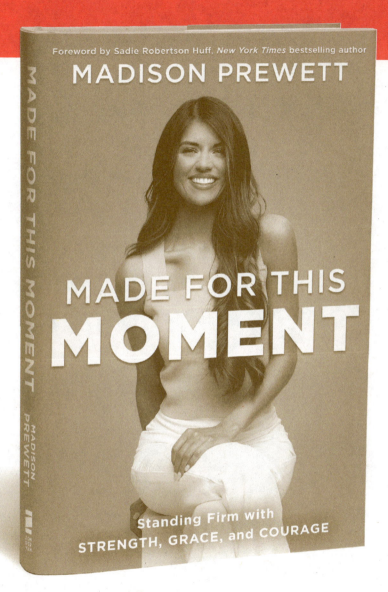

Available in stores and online!

MORE FROM

We hope you enjoyed this Bible study from **Madison Prewett Troutt**. Here are some other Bible studies we think you'll like.

Get Out Of Your Head
VIDEO STUDY

Jennie Allen

Forgiving What You Can't Forget
VIDEO STUDY

Lysa TerKeurst

Our Mission
Equipping people to understand the Scriptures, cultivate spiritual growth, and live an inspired faith with Bible study and video resources from today's most trusted voices.

Megan Fate Marshman

Meant For Good
VIDEO STUDY

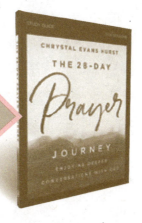

The 28-Day Prayer Journal
VIDEO STUDY

Chrystal Evans Hurst

Find your next Bible study, video series, or ministry training at:
HarperChristianResources.com

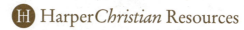

For churches, groups, and individuals

Want access to more great studies like this one? Subscribe now to get full access to the entire Study Gateway library!

StudyGateway.com

Powered by

Discover new studies

from teachers you love, and

new teachers

we know you'll love!

Explore all these teachers and more.

SHOP NOW

Kasey Van Norman

Chrystal Evans Hurst

Jada Edwards

Wendy Speake

Christine Caine

Ann Voskamp

Ruth Chou Simons

Bianca Olthoff

Shannon Bream

Dr. Anita Phillips

SAVE $10 on orders $50+! Use promo code **BIBLESTUDY12**

From the Publisher

GREAT STUDIES
ARE EVEN BETTER WHEN THEY'RE SHARED!

Help others find this study:

- Post a review at your favorite online bookseller.

- Post a picture on a social media account and share why you enjoyed it.

- Send a note to a friend who would also love it—or, better yet, go through it with them.

Thanks for helping others grow their faith!